Where are all these people going?

MARGE'S DINER

MARGE'S DINER

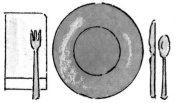

BY GAIL GIBBONS

THOMAS Y. CROWELL

NEW YORK

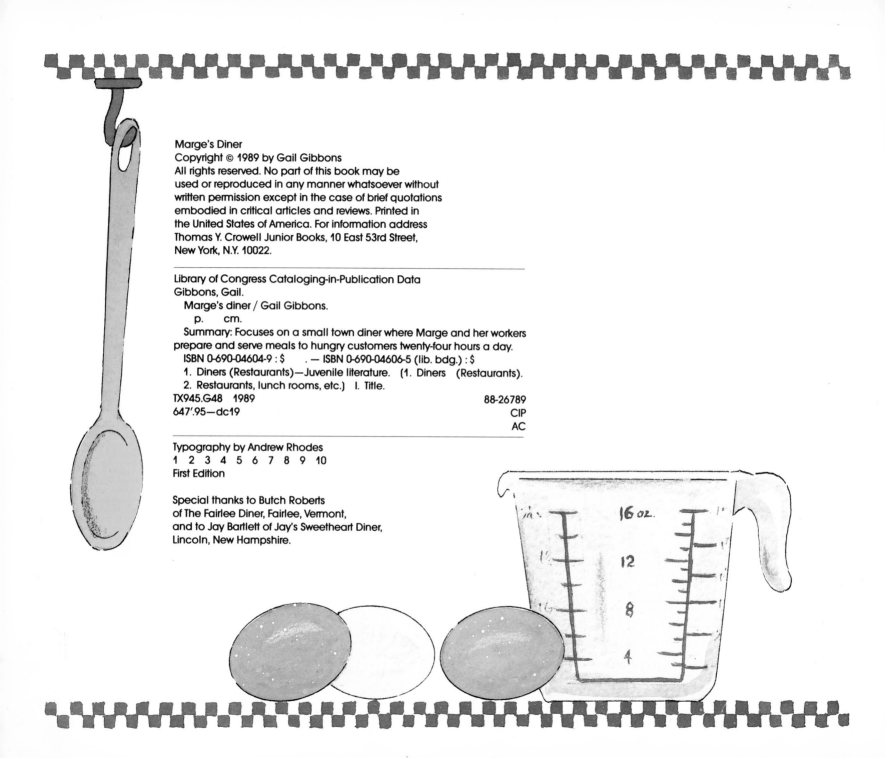

Library of Congress Cataloging-in-Publication Data
Gibbons, Gail.
  Marge's diner / Gail Gibbons.
    p.   cm.
  Summary: Focuses on a small town diner where Marge and her workers
prepare and serve meals to hungry customers twenty-four hours a day.
  ISBN 0-690-04604-9 : $. — ISBN 0-690-04606-5 (lib. bdg.) : $
  1. Diners (Restaurants)—Juvenile literature. (1. Diners (Restaurants).
  2. Restaurants, lunch rooms, etc.) I. Title.
TX945.G48 1989   88-26789
647'.95—dc19   CIP
                                                     AC

Typography by Andrew Rhodes
1 2 3 4 5 6 7 8 9 10
First Edition

Special thanks to Butch Roberts
of The Fairlee Diner, Fairlee, Vermont,
and to Jay Bartlett of Jay's Sweetheart Diner,
Lincoln, New Hampshire.

Everyone in town knows Marge.

She runs Marge's Diner.

Marge's Diner is open 24 hours a day.
You never can tell who you'll meet there.

The breakfast crowd starts coming in at seven o'clock.

Mr. Ross is in a hurry. He flips through his paper, sips a cup of coffee, and waits for his breakfast to be served.

A vacationing family comes in for a big breakfast. They'll be driving 300 miles before they stop again.

Joe has a truck route. He drives through town twice a week, and he always stops at Marge's. "Feels good to be off the highway," Joe says, climbing up on a stool. "I'll have my usual, Bill."

Bill, the short-order cook, is behind the counter. "Saw you coming—it's almost ready."

Marge has to feed all these people!

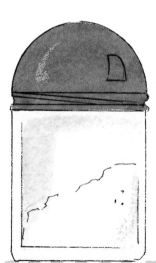

Bill is busy at the grill, frying bacon and sausages, flipping pancakes, and stirring hash browns. He can handle lots of different orders at once. Bill can even crack an egg with one hand!

The baker has been working since midnight, making muffins and doughnuts, cakes, and pies. Now her shift is over. "You've done it again!" Marge says. "Everything looks delicious. See you tomorrow."

Out front, breakfast is going just fine. It's still early, but Marge is already in the kitchen, preparing for lunch and dinner. A waitress rushes in with a tray full of dirty dishes. "We'd better have these washed right away, Marge," she warns. "It's really getting busy out there."

The diner is a cozy place. On cold mornings the windows steam up.
The smells of coffee, cinnamon buns, and sausages blend together.
At Marge's you can get good home cooking!

Bill pokes his head in the kitchen doorway. "Marge, can you give us a hand out front for a while?" When things get busy at the diner, everyone pitches in. They even take turns at the cash register.

When the breakfast rush is over, Bill sits down to have a cup of coffee.
This is the first break he's had all morning.

Marge takes her break at the same time. She sits in a booth, working on
bills. When a delivery truck pulls up out back, Marge's break is over.

It's almost noon. Bill prepares the grill and carries a batch of meatballs to the steam table. The waitresses refill the salt and pepper shakers and place fresh bottles of ketchup on each table. Marge writes the lunch specials on a chalkboard.

Now they are ready for the lunchtime crowd.

Mike, a policeman, comes in and swings onto one of the stools at the counter.

"Well, Mike, if you're here it must be 12:15," Bill says. "Your burger is already on the grill."

What a busy place—there's hardly an empty seat to be found!

A gang of construction workers go over some blueprints while they wait for lunch to be served.

A newspaper reporter eats his "soup of the day"—tomato!—and leafs through notes for a story.

For the past two weeks a telephone company crew has been repairing
cables nearby. Marge's Diner has become their favorite lunchtime spot.
"Hey, Marge," the crew boss says, "we think you make the best french fries
in town."

After a while, the lunchtime crowd thins out.

Now Marge has time to phone her suppliers with her weekly order. She needs 195 pounds of flour, 60 pounds of bacon, 125 pounds of sugar—plus sausage, chopped meat, vegetables, milk, eggs, ice cream, and more.

You use up lots of groceries when you feed as many people as Marge does!

One of the waitresses is printing the "blue plate special" on cards for tonight's dinner menus. She turns to the booth behind her. "Gee, you have a lot of books today, Molly."

Marge's daughter, Molly, comes in every day for an after-school snack. This time Marge brings her a steaming mug of hot chocolate. "Wow, have I got a ton of homework tonight," Molly gripes.

"Okay, you better get right to it. The booth is all yours," Marge says.

Soon the high-school crowd shows up. The diner is their favorite place to hang out. They drop quarters into the jukebox and turn the music up as loud as they can.

One of the girls orders a "kitchen-sink sundae"—it has everything! "Are you going to eat all that, Sue?" her friend teases.

Everyone talks at once:

"That's my favorite song. Don't you love it?"

"Can you believe that history assignment?"

"Are you going to the game on Saturday night?"

By five o'clock, Bill and the waitresses are ready to go home. They've been on their feet for hours. The night crew comes in to take over.

"Good night, Marge," Bill says. "Don't forget, we're having stew tomorrow. It's going to be another chilly day."

Marge is having an early dinner with her family. Marge's husband joins Marge and Molly at the diner every evening after work. Now's their chance to catch up on one another's news.

"I'll be home at my usual time," Marge tells them. "There are just a few things to finish up."

Once again the diner is crowded with customers. They study their menus—the diner has something for everyone!

One family stops in for a quick bite on their way to the movies. "Could we have our order taken right away, please? We're rushing to make the seven o'clock show."

At the next booth, Marge is ordering a Deluxe Dinner, "on the house," for Ned. "He's this week's winner of the jelly-bean contest," Marge says. "He guessed how many beans are in the jar."

Mr. Reynolds lives close to Marge's Diner. He comes in every night and orders the "blue plate special" for his supper. Marge and all her workers know him.

Today is a special day—Mr. Reynold's birthday. And Marge has a surprise for him.

"Happy birthday, Mr. Reynolds!" everyone shouts.
"I don't believe it," he exclaims. "How did you know?"

"Hope you like chocolate," Marge says with a wink.

At last things slow down. Marge checks her list of supplies for tomorrow.
Are there clean aprons? Are there enough paper napkins?

She takes a turkey out of the freezer to thaw. She goes over tomorrow's
menu. Marge was going to make mushroom soup, but the mushrooms
were never delivered. She decides to make pea soup instead.

It's time for Marge to leave.

"Remember, the floor waxers will be here later," Marge says.

All the money in the cash register has been counted. On her way home, Marge will make a night deposit at the bank.

Marge's day is finally over. She heads home, knowing that any late customers will be well taken care of by the night crew at Marge's Diner.